W9-BBG-671

Chicago Revisited

by John Gunther

Dedicated to
James Weber Linn and
Edith Foster Flint,
in absentia,
and to Earle Ludgin,
Trustee and Friend

Clearly there existed one person who could tell the story of The University of Chicago today with greater authority than anyone else.

For one thing, this man was an alumnus. His knowledge of the University had deep roots. He had lived through great developments on the campus. He would be immediately aware of new ones. His name was John Gunther, he was one of the world's most astute (and readable) reporters.

However, it was not with a very sanguine feeling that I dialed Mr. Gunther's New York telephone number. When President Beadle and I first called on him with an invitation to visit the University after an absence of many years and to write down what he found, in the manner (and with the candor) of his famous Inside *books, we could only feel that we had committed an imposition.*

Not that John Gunther was other than gracious. No man alive is more polite.

But it was apparent during our pleasant luncheon that this most affable gentleman was even then a fugitive from his publishers. There was a long overdue novel that he was in the throes of finishing. He was two magazine assignments behind; he had promised to go to South America to complete his contemporary political history of the continents. And the editors of Look *were breathing down his neck for an encyclopaedic piece on the course of the twentieth century.*

"I don't see how I can wedge in another thing," he said. Nor did we.

"Nevertheless," Mr. Gunther concluded, "telephone me

in a week. In the meantime I'll see if I can change any *of my plans."*

Even though we had impressed upon him that ours was a professional proposition, a bid at the highest price, it seemed entirely unlikely that Gunther could postpone such pressing commitments.

Imagine our delight then when he, himself, answered my telephone call and said eagerly, "I've been waiting to hear from you.

"I am bursting to tell you that while I can't possibly undertake the assignment we discussed, I am going to do it anyway!

"I only can't tell you the moment of my arrival. This we will shortly arrange."

And that we did.

The result of Mr. Gunther's visit to the campus and his conversations with faculty and students and friends, together with some severe critics of the University, appears in the following pages.

Despite our proposal that as a man who makes his living by writing he should be paid well ("we pay our doctors," we said), John Gunther refused any payment at all.

"This," he said, "is a labor of love. Besides, you may not like what I write."

Of course we did.

We trust that you will, too.

FAIRFAX M. CONE
Chairman of the Board of Trustees
The University of Chicago

Chicago Revisited

Preface

The University of Chicago often reminds me of one of those peculiar miniature principalities which still survive in Europe, like Liechtenstein, Andorra, or San Marino, although there is nothing trivial about it. Or it might be compared to a medieval city-state, tenaciously keeping up its status as an independent and somewhat isolated community while maintaining close, intricate relations with the surrounding countryside. The University of Chicago has, one might say, its own nationalism. It has a special tang and color, quite without regard to the State of Illinois or the City of Chicago, its hinterland. It has its own foreign policy (there has been trouble on its frontiers) and, like governments, it faces problems in demography, finance, and personnel. It has its own structure of power politics, and is served by a thoroughly competent president, secretary of state, and cabinet. Recently it even had to fight a war, which it won, but by a narrow squeak.

In a long professional life I have tackled the job of writing about a good many nations, cities, and institutions, and I have always sought to ask a number of questions:

What does this place look like?

Where did it come from?

What are its prevailing qualities and characteristics?

Who runs it?

Is the population satisfied?

Where is it going?

In this survey I will try to do the same thing for the University of Chicago.

I myself happen to be a Chicago alumnus, but this does not mean that I am necessarily prejudiced in its favor. I have not been a good alumnus, nor was I a particularly good undergraduate; I was rude enough to decamp a month or so before graduation, and never attended a convocation. Never once have I attended an alumni reunion. Then, out of the blue, came an invitation to take a look at the University after the lapse of many years, and, mostly because of the persuasive power and charm of those who conveyed it, I accepted with alacrity.

This is what I found.

Leaded Windows and Glass Walls

Irrefragably independent, tough minded, and even haughty as this principality may be, it is a small principality, dominating an area whose borders measure about a mile and a half by a mile. The actual campus covers some 184 acres, on which stand no fewer than 110 buildings. Thanks to the developing national impulse for urban renewal, Chicago shares with all major urban universities modest hopes for expansion—and probably will have about as much difficulty as the others in finding the space it will need to survive. With the aid of the city administration, the University has acquired 26.5 acres of additional land from a reclaimed slum area so that it can expand its South Campus. The population is small as well, numbering about 20,000 in all. There are 1,035 full-time faculty members, practically all of whom have the Ph.D. or equivalent degree, 480 research associates, and 131 teachers in the University's pre-collegiate school system (Chicago will take a child from the age of three!). The ratio of teachers to students is roughly one to eight, a high proportion.

Quality at an academic institution cannot be built merely upon individual brilliance. First rate work and first rate people need support both broad and deep. At Chicago, the faculty is supported by a staff of 8,024 (including 1,300 part-time student workers). This makes the University one of the ten largest employers within the central city.

The student body on the Midway campus numbers only about 8,300. In these days of "multiversities" this is a very small figure. It actually is less than the average *freshman* enrollment at several great state universities in the Middle West. But the University of Chicago, a particular kind of institution, has no interest in largeness for its own sake. A pearl is more valuable than a baseball. And the University still carries its original note of freshness, elevation, and, above all, quality.

Freshness . . . elevation . . . quality—these attributes are also evident in the person of George W. Beadle, the University's president since 1960. Trustees and faculty members who helped persuade him to leave California for Chicago were effusive in their praise of him. Their report urging his appointment said they were "impressed by his personal qualities of modesty, integrity, analytical ability, decisive and direct response and action, and the breadth of his scholarly understanding." George Beadle is a sharp contrast to the stereotyped academic administrator. He commands international respect as a man of science, serves on many distinguished committees, writes scores of longhand letters weekly to interesting people around the world and still finds time to give twelve hours a day, at least, to the affairs of a great university.

I hope that alumni and others close to the University will forgive me if I take a paragraph or two to describe its physical plant, which they probably know better than I do. I spent some rewarding hours wandering around old haunts. The main campus has changed little since I first saw it. It has, so to speak, been filled in, but the central design, the basic structure and pattern as laid down by the first builders, remains intact. It is still a handsomely self-contained community of lawns and quadrangles, the battlements of which are built of gray Indiana limestone in the Gothic manner. The gargoyles, ivy, spires, apertures, red slate, scrolled designs, look mildly anachronistic, but are pleasing. Mitchell Tower, which is modeled on the Tower at Magdalen College, Oxford, still has a luminous sheen, and so does Hutchinson Commons, built on the plan of Christ Church Hall, Oxford. I have always thought that Hutchinson was the most beautiful building on campus.

Mandel Hall, which was the chapel of my day, serves now as a chamber for jazz concerts and lectures by individuals as vastly divergent as James Baldwin, with all his protesting fire, and an Illinois product like the late Adlai E. Stevenson, so immaculately distinguished. (It isn't difficult to remember the number of seats in Mandel Hall. There are 1,066—the same number as the year of the Norman invasion of Britain.)

The Chicago area comprises the largest Roman Catholic archdiocese in the United States. In the spring of 1964 the Divinity School—an outstanding center of Protestant theological teaching and research—invited a renowned "liberal" Roman Catholic cardinal to deliver two major lectures in Mandel Hall. The seminars and long informal chats which Leon-Josef Cardinal Suenens, Archbishop of Malines-Brussels and Primate of Belgium, held with faculty members and students made news with quite an impact. His successful visit encouraged Dean Jerald C. Brauer (a brilliant young Lutheran) in his planning to establish a special chair of Roman Catholic Life and Thought on the Divinity School faculty.

The chapel which superseded Mandel Hall, and which is the only building on the campus named for John D. Rockefeller (who gave the University the fantastic sum of $35 million from first to last) has a tower rising to 207 feet, and tradition has it that no building on the campus may ever be built higher. The doors of this chapel formerly stood open at all hours, but nowadays they close at 5:00 P.M. A wisecrack attributed to a former president of the University has it that, in the evening, it became a citadel for the romantically inclined, and more souls were conceived than saved there.

Several of the newer buildings are not, I noticed, quite so unchallengeably Gothic as their predecessors. One reason for this is window washing. Gothic, however modified, is a style notorious for its use of small, odd-shaped leaded windows which have proved difficult and expensive to keep clean. And the University has no fewer than 35,000 windows to wash twice a year.

Grass too is a problem. It is the cause of the principal running gag on the campus associated with President Beadle. He likes grass, as becomes a native of the Nebraska plain, and to save the lawns, he caused to be set up fragile low fences, only a foot high and consisting of a single strand of rope, at points where students took short cuts which ruined the lawns. After all, the University has 172,500 square feet of cement walks. But nothing, it seems, can make youngsters content to use them and Beadle's fences are ignored with the result that the President is subject to a continual amiable assault of jokes and jibes. "Well, it takes their minds off football," one dean sighed.

South Campus, across the green shallow trough of the Midway Plaisance, has architecture quite different from the main campus. Here we leave Gothic behind. The works of three major modern architects stand in order along a "cultural mile," arrayed like specimens to be savored at leisure by the architectural connoisseur. Eero Saarinen designed the Law School, with black glass walls which seem pleated; the Center for Continuing Education, with its gentle columns, is the work of Edward Durell Stone; and Ludwig Mies van der Rohe is responsible for the brilliant, provocative School of Social Service Administration. A new dormitory complex (on the other side of the campus) is also by Saarinen.

Behind the imposing façade to the south lies a belt of slum which is of continuing concern to the University, to city officials, and to the citizens of Chicago. The University administration is working with civic groups, urban planners, and local authorities to make this area as flourishing a section of Chicago as the Hyde Park–Kenwood community to the north.

Question. Elucidation. Discussion.

Looking at the University anew after many years' absence, I wanted first of all to find out something about the rockbottom citizenry of this principality, this city-state—in other words, the undergraduates. Of course the University of Chicago is, and always has been since its foundation in 1890, primarily a graduate school—a bastion for archers and men with catapults, not the junior infantry. And in fact students working for advanced degrees and those in the graduate professional schools outnumber undergraduates today by a ratio of two to one.

The University acquires as undergraduates the scholastic cream of the cream. It has appeal for all sorts of bright youngsters, and especially favors vigorous "achievers" with serious motives and imaginative, independent turns of mind. Director of Admissions Charles O'Connell every year conducts a nationwide grass roots campaign to find emerging talent in rural high schools—and the academic performance of these recruits more than justifies the effort and expense of locating them. Chicago students come from farms and hamlets, from slums and suburbia. Although they study in the lee of a great graduate school, the College students are not repelled by their more mature and more extensively educated colleagues—instead, they are attracted. Chicago is not an obvious place for the average student, but gifted youngsters find it supremely challenging, and some others discover abilities they never knew they had. Six foreign countries and forty-four states were represented in one recent class.

Chicago has been famous for years as a fine city to stay away from. This is partly because it is supposed to have a vile climate. Actually, the weather here is much better in both winter and summer than New York's, and far more pleasant in summer than that of Washington or Los Angeles. Another common complaint about Chicago stems from the Capone days, and the fact that New York and Los Angeles long ago took the lead from Chicago in most kinds of criminal activity has not changed the popular notion.

The city does have attractions for many people,

and one of the greatest of these is the University of Chicago. In a recent year, for example, the 745 graduate students who were given advanced degrees came from 190 different colleges and universities. Indeed the population of this city-state is variegated.

They had come, literally, from everywhere: from Harvard, Yale and Princeton; from Vassar, Bryn Mawr, Wellesley and Radcliffe; from Swarthmore, Oberlin, Haverford, Reed, and Antioch; from Dartmouth and Williams; from M.I.T. and C.I.T., Rensselaer Poly, and Georgia Tech.

They had come from the four corners of the United States: from Maine's Bates and Bowdoin, and the University of Florida and Miami University of the East Coast; and from California and Stanford, U.C.L.A., Claremont, Oregon, and Washington on the West Coast; from N.Y.U., Columbia, and C.C.N.Y.; from Penn State, Ohio State, Michigan State, and Iowa State; also the state universities of Wisconsin, Indiana, Illinois, Minnesota, Colorado, Arizona, Kansas, Connecticut, Vermont, Kentucky, Massachusetts, Maryland, North Carolina, Delaware, Missouri, Wyoming, and South Dakota.

They had come from Notre Dame and Holy Cross, from St. Mary's and St. Joseph's; from St. Lawrence and St. John; from Cornell, Colgate, Rochester, and Syracuse; from Brown and Boston and Baylor; from Emory, Bethel, Vanderbilt, Duke, Southern Methodist, and the University of the

South; from Kenyon and Western Reserve; from Washington and Jefferson, and Franklin and Marshall.

They had come from Andrews, Augustana, Butler, Berea, Calvin, Duchesne, Earlham, Hiram, Lawrence, Lehigh, Macalester, Norwich, St. Louis, St. Olaf's, Trinity, Tulane, Transylvania, Valparaiso, Walla Walla, and Brigham Young.

They had come from Canada: from the University of Toronto and McGill University, from Manitoba University, the University of British Columbia, and Queens University of Kingston, Ontario.

They had come from Oxford and Cambridge and the University of London; from the University of Tokyo and Tokyo Agricultural University, from Keio University and Okayama University in Japan; from National Chekiang University in Hangchow, China, and the Union Theological University and Far Eastern University of Manila; from the University of Belgrade, the University of Zurich, Ludwig Maximilian University in Munich, and the University of Debrecen in Hungary; also Rhodes in South Africa, the University of Ankara in Turkey, the University of Calcutta, Patna University of India, Agra University at Indore, the University of Mysore, and the American University at Beirut, Lebanon.

They had come from the University of Adelaide in Australia; from National Taiwan University in Taipei; from Seoul National University in Korea;

from the University of Puerto Rico; and from Queens College, Belfast, Ireland.

There were sixty-two others, but this will prove to you, as it did to me, that there is nothing provincial about Chicago's Midway.

Interestingly, several faculty members whom I met expressed mild displeasure at the special quality of Chicago undergraduates. They would like to have fewer eggheads, more hell-raisers, to give the College community better balance, although nobody wants to make it a charm or glamor school. Be this as it may, the quality of the average Chicago undergraduate is remarkable. Of a recent freshman class eighty-two per cent ranked in the top ten per cent of their high school senior classes; twenty-seven were National Merit Scholars.

No quota system of any kind governs entrance to the University. No questions are asked on application forms about race or religion, and a photograph is optional. About half the undergraduate body has help in the form of scholarships, and nearly two-thirds have part-time jobs of one sort or another. The average scholarship for an entering freshman is $1,400, and the University spends about $10 million a year on various forms of aid to College and graduate students.

Of course University of Chicago grads were bright in my day too, but not as terrifyingly bright as today's leaders seem to be. I noticed some other changes:

1. A married student was a great rarity in the 1920's; today of course this is common not only at the U. of C. but all over the country.

2. Undergraduate social life was almost entirely dominated by the Greek-letter fraternities although, even then, the fraternity system was not so all-embracing as at other middle-western schools.

3. In my day a large percentage of students came from the Chicago area and lived at home. Now the institution has become almost completely a residential college; residence on the campus is, in fact, obligatory for one year for all men, and for two years for women. Almost as many undergraduates come from the New York area as from Chicago; only twenty-five per cent of a recent class came from Illinois.

4. Student government is much stronger (I am not sure that this even existed in my time).

One professor put it to me that the campus still boiled with "impassioned cliques," but surely this is a healthy sign. Another said that the chief distinguishing mark of the contemporary student was his vivid capacity for "enthusiasm—which he would go to any length to hide!" The gist of the matter is that students want to be part of the policy-making activity of the University as a whole. They like to negotiate with faculty committees, have a hand in decisions about curricula, and be able to give effective voice to complaints ranging from the scarcity of coffee dispensing machines to "the moldy half thought" of some members of the faculty.

Be this as it may, the unique population of the tiny Chicago principality enjoys some remarkable opportunities. Many of these are extracurricular. During the two weeks of my visit, for example, there were sessions open to all students ranging from lectures on "Galileo and His Contemporaries" to such entertainments as "Bogey Flicks," a continuing series of motion pictures starring the thin-lipped, sardonic Mr. Humphrey Bogart, and varsity baseball, golf, and tennis.

Bogart, Bacall, *et al.* are to watch at the University of Chicago. Varsity baseball, football, golf, and tennis are to play. When Chicago resigned from the Big Ten, the idea was not to renounce athletics but rather to repudiate the idea of sports in the arena where all but a handful of the participants are lookers-on. Intramural sports are decidedly "in" on the Midway.

I spent one afternoon with four bright, knowledgeable undergraduates. One was a vice-president of the Student Government; another, a Negro, was editor of the *Maroon* (the campus newspaper, circulation 10,000). These youngsters, one of whom was a pretty blonde girl who seemed to be appallingly young, but who was specializing in Russian Civilization and had already had her first extensive trip in the Soviet Union, impressed and puzzled me. They were very guarded—perhaps shy. I asked them what they liked most about the University.

Well, it was one hell of a good *school.* They did not feel at all that they, as undergraduates, were overshadowed by the prevailing emphasis on graduate study. Quite the contrary—they were being amply prepared for graduate work. Complaints? First, tuition charges were too high. They wanted to get at the bottom of the accounting system used by the University and see why costs could not be reduced. Second, the general education courses were sometimes "badly" taught and did not reach fully enough into the present. They wanted more emphasis on the contemporary, particularly in history and the humanities. (Incidentally, if my search through the catalogues bore correct fruit, only one man living is honored with a whole course—Stravinsky, and this is given in the graduate division, not the College.) Third, the University was behind the times in its approach to the racial problem. Fourth, although they freely conceded that the University was thoroughly liberal, youngsters *could* get into trouble by being overvociferous on civil rights, censorship, and so on. Recently a minor fight took place because a student publication serialized *The Naked Lunch,* by William Burroughs. Fifth, intelligent youngish teachers might, my informants said, be in danger of being fired just before they got tenure if they did not "conform."

I did not inquire into every student complaint, of course. Some comments seemed to be emotional and subjective. The complaint about "badly taught" courses probably reflected the incredibly high standards which the idealism of youth sometimes entertains; I have heard similar complaints about professors at Cambridge, Oxford, and Harvard. The point here seemed to be that the students really cared about the quality of teaching—and so, many faculty members assured me, did the teachers.

I did look into some of the objective questions raised by the students I met. For instance, it appeared to be true that there were comparatively few Negro undergraduates. But there are as many at Chicago, I daresay, as might be found at other equally expensive universities maintaining equally Spartan entrance requirements. Expense is only a small part of the story; substantial financial aid usually can be provided for the deserving student who needs it. The most important factor, as colleges across the land are discovering, is that secondary school education available to minority groups has proved inadequate to the demands of the prestige universities and thus has provided few qualified Negro applicants. Nevertheless, Chicago can boast that one of its most illustrious alumni is Dr. Hastings Banda, Prime Minister of Malawi, who received his undergraduate degree in the thirties. Several prominent Negro professors were appointed to tenure positions on Chicago's faculty long before desegregation became a burning national issue. John Hope Franklin, a Harvard-educated Negro who has become one of the nation's leading historians on the Reconstruction, has joined Chicago's faculty after teaching at Cambridge as a visiting professor.

It was difficult to determine precisely what the students meant by such phrases as "getting into trouble" and "conform." I certainly did not get the impression that Chicago has an oppressed student body. In the civil rights field alone, several national leaders of CORE (Congress of Racial Equality) and SNCC (Student Non-Violent Coordinating Committee) once were students at Chicago.

I doubt that a professor ever has been fired at Chicago for "non-conformity," despite what students may say loosely. In my interviews with them, faculty members were generous in their praise for the freedom and independence they are granted by the administration of the University. If there is pressure on them, it probably is the social pressure of the academic community to work hard, teach well, and contribute in positive terms to mankind's storehouse of usable knowledge. I heard the dictum "publish or perish" quoted lightheartedly over luncheons at the faculty club.

The next day I climbed the old iron stairway of Cobb Hall and sat in on a sophomore humanities course. No rostrum, no desks. Eleven young men, ten young women sat informally with an instructor around a large oval table. Classes are commendably small—averaging eighteen—at Chicago. A blackboard carried a "No Smoking" sign but three or four students smoked cigarettes and the instructor sucked on a pipe. The class was reading Plato's *Gorgias,* and instruction took the form of questions, elucidation, and discussion. The mood was nicely—but not exaggeratedly—spirited. There are all manner of innovations at Chicago. Formal lectures usually do not take place more than once a week, and only original texts are used. At examinations the identity of the student is unknown to the examiner who goes over his papers.

The curriculum has changed vastly and for the good. When I went to Chicago I was obliged to take only *two* courses (and each for only a single quarter) in my entire four years of work for a bachelor's degree—English Composition and Shakespeare. Outside of these two, I was pretty well free to roam as I pleased providing I took enough courses in English, my major. This was in the 1920's—a period of electivism gone wild. As a result I was never subjected to a proper educational process at all. Mostly I took what I liked and what was easiest. I was never compelled to spend a single hour in four years on a foreign language. I was permitted to graduate—with honors—without ever having had more than the barest minimum of economics, political science, philosophy, or sociology, and nothing at all in music or the arts. I never had five minutes in classics, religion, geography, geology, archeology, anthropology, or any biological science at all. All I did was read English and history (my minor) and have a bit of chemistry and math.

This was, by hindsight, a scandalous system—but one widely used then throughout the country. It has been stopped at Chicago. Nowadays the advocates of general education are listened to with respect. This, indeed, next to the quarter system which has been widely copied (and will surely be introduced in many more universities), is still one of Chicago's distinctive excellences in the undergraduate realm today. The alert, bright-eyed early careerists receive an excellent pre-professional education and often move rapidly toward their chosen goals. But the University makes it clear that it values the well-rounded person, with a solid underpinning of general knowledge, before specialization begins. What the University wants to stress is the "interrelation of disciplines" and thus arose the now celebrated broad-beam courses (don't call them "surveys"!) which every student is obliged to take and which occupy one-fourth of his total studies, whatever his major.

The four obligatory courses are: Humanities, Biological Sciences, Physical Sciences, and Social Sciences.

But, beyond these four, there are additional requirements in general education for the student, dependent upon his major subject. If a student is majoring in English, as an example, he must have another year-long course in Humanities (other than English); another in Social Sciences or one of the natural sciences; History of Western Civilization; two years of a foreign language; a senior seminar in Humanities; and free electives outside of his major. His work in English, which is itself a program built on a solid structure with several parts, occupies about one-fourth of his total studies.

One should also mention that instruction in the fourth year may be tutorial, and that "specialization" does not mean vocational education. Chicago is certainly not the place to go to study ice-cream manufacture or hotel management.

About 300 members of the faculty specifically serve the undergraduate body, but practically all professors, no matter how elevated, may teach in the College. Many, including President Beadle, like to do so, because it gives them the chance to associate with fresh, youthful minds.

Realms of the Recondite

Now we approach the higher ramparts of the Chicago principality—the graduate divisions and the graduate professional schools. The graduate divisions are the Humanities (roughly 875 students), Biological Sciences excluding medicine (330), Physical Sciences (575), and Social Sciences (1,450). Here are enticing realms of the recondite; courses exist from Balkan Linguistics to Neuropharmacology. Here, too, in spite of close emphasis on the refinements of particularized scholarship, we find that some of the frontiers between disciplines have already broken down—particularly in the sciences. The University encourages this. There are professors who scarcely know whether they belong to one department or another. Nobody knows these days where biology stops and physics starts. Here, too, the relations of professor to student can attain an exquisite level of intellectual intimacy. The Department of Music, one of the strongest on the campus and one of the most seminal and stimulating in the country, has a staff of twelve for fifty music majors. Astronomy presently has eleven teachers, including several men of formidable renown, for sixteen graduate students.

Many universities today have a tendency to be choosy about students who apply for graduate work. Chicago takes a more liberal attitude and prides itself for its hospitality to "risk" admissions; it will take a chance on a bright boy, no matter how spotty or unconventional his previous education has been. Some of these have paid off well. And, of course, undergrads from Chicago itself are encouraged to proceed. In fact more than seventy-five per cent of those receiving bachelor degrees go on to pursue advanced work; according to a recent survey, a higher proportion of Chicago undergraduates progressed to earn a doctorate between 1921 and 1961 than in any other university in the country.

Needless to say, the graduate and professional schools spawn an enormous amount of talent. Chicago ranks as the nation's largest per capita producer of college and university teachers in the nation. It is an incubator, a teacher of teachers. In one recent year, no fewer than 167 presidents of other American colleges or universities—one out of ten—either are Chicago alumni, or have been faculty members—an almost unbelievable statistic.

The University has 73,000 living alumni, many of these distinguished in various fields. I don't want this pamphlet to bristle unduly with statistics, but surely it should be mentioned that one out of every fifteen men in *American Men of Science* is a Chicago man; one out of every eleven in *Leaders of Education,* one out of every ten in the *Directory of American Scholars.* In 1962 the American Physical Society chose more Chicago Ph.D.'s for membership (97 out of 1,138) than those of any other university.

Quite apart from the graduate divisions, the student at Chicago has a choice of seven professional schools—Business, Divinity, Education, Law, Library, Medicine, and Social Service Administration. Then, too, there are such notable facilities as the Enrico Fermi Institute for Nuclear Studies, the Institute for the Study of Metals, the Laboratory for Astrophysics and Space Research, the pre-collegiate schools (founded by John Dewey), a Center for Continuing Education, a Department of Biophysics, and an Institute for Computer Research. When a hopeful friend tried to explain the work done by this last I did not understand a single word; one of its monstrous tools bears the splendid name MANIAC III. But I had a wonderfully illuminating afternoon at the Sonia Shankman Orthogenic School, which is devoted to the study and rehabilitation of emotionally disturbed children. Here Professor Bruno Bettelheim, the survivor of a Nazi concentration camp who is a scholar in three different Chicago departments (education, psychiatry, and psychology) explained the extraordinary subtleties of his work in repairing the broken mental health of children, and told me the life histories of some he has reclaimed—introducing me to them, too.

Then the University operates Yerkes Observatory in Wisconsin, and, in conjunction with the University of Texas, the McDonald Observatory in Fort Davis, Texas. Its Oriental Institute maintains Chicago House in Luxor, Egypt.

The Law School, which takes in no more than 160 students a year out of an average of 1,400 who apply, is incontestably one of the foremost in the nation. Its graduates form an elite all over the country, not merely as practicing lawyers but as judges, teachers, and servants of the government. It has its own courtroom and its own legal aid clinic, and its *Law Review* has been cited in at least fifteen recent Supreme Court decisions. Max Rheinstein is the world's outstanding scholar in the field of comparative law. The Law School continues to attract top scholars to its faculty from other leading institutions; recent additions are Geoffrey Hazard from the University of California and Grant Gilmore from the School of Law at Yale.

The Graduate School of Business has a similar prestige and reputation. With a faculty of eighty-three and a student body on campus of 580, it is the second oldest American business school, having been founded in 1898. Its techniques differ sharply from those of most business schools; it does not concentrate so much on how to make money fast or on current business practice as on long range principles and theory. The Divinity School, with an illustrious tradition going back to William Rainey Harper, graduates more Ph.D.'s than any similar school in the nation, and the Library School was the first one in the country to give the Ph.D. for research in library science.

Chicago has always been a pioneer not merely in theoretical sociology but in its practical application to immediate urban problems. One research landmark is a series of forty-four books and monographs, published by sociologists trained at Chicago, which constitutes the first large-scale empirical investigation of the social characteristics of modern cities. Demographers in the department can practically tell you what the population of Indianapolis will be at 10:05 A.M. on July 17, 2093.

The School of Medicine is an integral part of the Division of Biological Sciences, and medical students at Chicago have exceptional opportunities. There are 781 scientists and doctors in the

Division; however, the freshman class in the School of Medicine is limited to seventy-two students every year. Eleven hospitals and clinics stand on the campus as integrated parts of the University. One is Lying-in Hospital. Another is the Argonne Cancer Research Hospital, which pioneered in "atomic" medicine. None of the staff of the University medical center is permitted to engage in private practice or to accept fees. They are full-time, full-salaried University personnel devoted only to the care of patients, research, and instruction in the campus hospitals and clinics. Patients come from everywhere, not merely the campus.

The list of celebrated physicians associated with the University is endless. It goes from Dr. Jacques Loeb, one of the fathers of modern medicine, and Dr. Alexis Carrel, a Nobel Prize winner in 1912, to the contemporary Dr. Charles B. Huggins, who won the Nobel Prize in 1966 for his discovery of a hormonal therapy for cancer of the prostate.

The Graduate School of Education, established in 1958, is the newest of Chicago's professional schools. But the University from the beginning has won renown for its research in education. Research is translated into direct service through a number of Centers in the education school—the Reading Research Center, the Urban Child Center, and the Comparative Education Center which investigates the differences in teaching and learning the world over. Since 1957 the University has been providing educational training and guidance in Pakistan, and for Pakistanis on the Chicago campus.

The Laboratory Schools, as the name implies, serve both as a demonstration center for effective teaching—from nursery school through twelve years of pre-college education—and as a research tool for testing and validating educational theory. Incidentally, the average I.Q. of the 1,700 students in the Lab Schools is higher than 130—not surprising, I suppose, since about half of them are children of University faculty members.

The Chicago student in the graduate divisions or graduate professional schools has, amongst much else, two particularly ample reservoirs of power to help sustain him—the library (equally open to undergrads), and an admirable and a well-established University Press if he becomes a scholar and wishes to publish. The Harper Memorial Library, ably directed by Herman H. Fussler, with 2.5 million volumes, is one of the great repositories of learning in the country. One detail is that it subscribes to no fewer than 8,000 different periodicals. But the library was built many years ago and even though about half its books are presently stacked in libraries of the separate departments, it is crowded to the seams; new facilities are imperative and planning for these has already begun. The Joseph Regenstein Library, an $18,000,000 graduate research facility, will be constructed. Something like three million books will be deposited in the Regenstein Library. They will include several magnificent special collections of value to scholars the world over. The present building will be converted into an open-shelf library for undergraduates. Another problem has to do with content. The prevailing thought is that the University should maintain its interdisciplinary tradition and faith in the unity of knowledge and concentrate all its library facilities into a central system, thus replacing the departmental libraries which exist today. But some departments, mathematics for one, want libraries all their own. Mathematicians always make problems.

Being a writer, I like publishers and presses and I enjoyed my visit to the University of Chicago Press. Its Princetonian director, Roger W. Shugg, is a professor turned publisher who came to his present post from a long experience in both university teaching and commercial publishing. The University of Chicago Press, founded in 1892, is the largest academic press in the country. Three learned journals it founded seventy years ago are still very much alive—the *Journal of Political Economy*, the *Journal of Geology*, and the *Journal of Near Eastern Studies* (then called *Hebraica*); now it publishes no fewer than thirty-one scholarly magazines and learned reviews which range in number of subscribers from 900 (*Physiological Zoölogy*) to 16,200 (*Elementary School Journal*). Altogether the Press has published more than 4,000 books, of which

1,600 are currently in print—a remarkable record. So many books have been outstanding that it is difficult to choose the leaders, but the Edgar J. Goodspeed translation of the *New Testament* has sold more than a million copies. Recent lively successes have been *The Road to Serfdom,* a conservative economic statement by Friedrich A. Von Hayek which has been called "God's answer to Stuart Chase," and *Atoms in the Family,* Laura Fermi's charming memoir of her husband, the Nobel laureate who first produced a chain reaction and thus inaugurated the atomic age on the University campus in 1942.

Chicago's faculty isn't perishing and it is publishing. Names from Chicago appear in popular book reviews as well as learned journals. Among faculty works in a recent Press catalogue are *Asia in the Making of Europe: The Century of Discovery,* by Donald F. Lach, Professor of Modern History; *The Heritage of Sociology,* a series edited by Morris Janowitz, Professor of Sociology; and *Ibn Khaldûn's Philosophy of History,* by Muhsin Mahdi, Professor of Arabic. A recent popular success was naturalist George B. Schaller's *The Year of the Gorilla.*

Of course many faculty members choose to have their books brought out by non-academic publishers, and this is all to the good. Viking published *Herzog,* the remarkable novel by Saul Bellow, Professor of Letters, and Atheneum brought out *The*

Image, or What Happened to the American Dream, by Daniel J. Boorstin, the Preston and Sterling Morton Professor in the Department of History.

Apart from its size, the most unusual thing about the Press is its relation to the University. From the beginning it has been a statutory academic division of the University not a mere adjunct or auxiliary enterprise. This was one of the unprecedented concepts of William Rainey Harper. There were few university presses at work in the 1890's, but Harper saw that no modern university could fulfill its purpose without having within it an active, well supported, well managed, and autonomous publishing division.

Illustrations abound. Let me be historical for a moment. Back in 1922 Dr. Nathaniel Kleitman, working in the "sleep lab," devised an electronic technique for tracing the eye movements of patients so that they could be awakened and given the opportunity to record their dreams, which would otherwise be forgotten. This was described in Kleitman's book, *Sleep and Wakefulness,* published by the Press and still in print. Longer ago, back in 1896, the philosopher John Dewey, who was then a member of the University faculty, conceived the idea of the "laboratory school" for primary school children. The institution he founded still exists, and his book, *The School and Society,* which describes it, has been selling steadily for more than sixty years. Albert A. Michelson, Professor of Physics and the first American scientist ever to receive a Nobel Prize, succeeded in measuring the speed of light in 1907; two of his books published by the Press still have a substantial sale in paperback. In 1921 Chicago Orientalists began work on an Assyrian dictionary. Thirty-five years and $800,000 later, as the Press puts it, the first volume was complete. Ten have now been compiled, and eleven more are to come. And, speaking of dictionaries, Sir William Craigie, the eminent Oxford lexicographer, joined the Chicago faculty in 1925 to direct the completion of the first *Dictionary of American English.* It took him until 1937 to finish Part One—"A" to "Baggage." When, two decades later, the four volumes were finally completed, they were a sellout at $100.

Incessant Speculation

Men—real men—stride along the thoroughfares of this academic commonwealth. What makes the University of Chicago great is neither endowment nor equipment, but men—the faculty. And by this criterion Chicago is, by almost unanimous consent, one of the three or four greatest universities in the world.

Twenty-eight Nobel Prize winners, some of whom I have already mentioned, have been associated with the University in one way or another so far; eight of these were alumni, like James D. Watson, a recent winner in medicine and physiology, who earned a Bachelor of Philosophy degree in the

College. In fact, Watson is a graduate of the U. of C. *nursery* school. In 1963 two of the three Nobel Prizes in physics and one of the two in chemistry went to former Chicago scientists. In 1966 two Nobel Prizes went to present members of the Chicago faculty—Dr. Charles B. Huggins for physiology and medicine, and Robert S. Mulliken for chemistry. Then, too, twenty-nine members of the faculty are members of the National Academy of Sciences, thirty-eight are fellows of the American Academy of Arts and Sciences, and nineteen are members of the American Philosophic Society, the oldest learned society in the country.

I lunched several times at the Quadrangle Club, the inner heart of faculty social life and intellectual interchange. This institution, now as always, is a vital asset to the University. It gives a pleasantly concrete though miniature image of what a university should, by standard definition, be—namely a *community* of scholars. The physicists tend to keep a bit aloof, but Egyptologists chat with musicians and a specialist in Henry Adams may be found arguing with a biologist. At one lunch I sat with a geophysicist, a professor of law, and a specialist in metals; at another the guests were a biophysicist, the chairman of the Department of History, and a political scientist, the redoubtable Hans J. Morgenthau.

Seventy per cent of the faculty live close enough to the University to be able to walk to their classrooms, an important factor in maintaining the community spirit, and their children by and large go to the same schools and play together. Nobody pulls rank; everybody from the President down is plain "Mr.," except Doctors of Medicine. There is no taboo on shop talk, and the general atmosphere is one of "critical sophistication." Some extremely queer fish exist among the eggheads. Brains, as I heard a trustee put it, don't care what kind of man they belong to. This faculty is a tough, free-wheeling set of super-specialists, built on individualism and quality, not the product of a mass-production line.

Professors at the University of Chicago have several advantages. (1) Salaries are high, as high as at Harvard or California, perhaps even higher. The average salary of a full professor is more than $21,000 a year, including fringe benefits. (2) The teaching load is probably lighter than in any other American university, six hours a week, or perhaps only three. This naturally makes the University a magnet for scholars who are encouraged to give as much of their time as possible to research. There are some formidable men of learning who never even hold formal classes. (3) No particular teaching rules apply, and the organizational structure is light. A professor has a very flexible position; he can create or drop a course almost at will. Moreover, Chicago is famous for giving teachers unlimited time for a project (for instance in the humanities) without interference. The University will wait ten years, twenty, thirty, for a job to be well done. (4) Academic liberties are enormously respected, contact with stimulating minds is assured, the level of intellectual energy is high, and, above all, the atmosphere is free.

Tenure, I discovered, is a complicated subject. A man starting at the bottom in Chicago, not somebody in midpassage seized in a raid from another university (raids and cross raids are a frequent phenomenon today all over the country), will normally serve four years as an instructor, six years as an assistant professor. Then, having completed ten years, he either must leave or become an associate professor and thus achieve tenure, which means that he cannot be fired except for gross misconduct.

Chicago does not give sabbaticals. This also is true of several other American universities, like Caltech. Instead, the man who wants to get away for a year can more or less take leave when his campus commitments are fulfilled.

Several friends lamented to me what they called the passage of the titans. Where, they asked, are men equivalent to Shorey (classics), Stagg (football), Small (the founder of modern sociology), Dodd (the historian who became ambassador to Germany), Werner Jaeger (Greek studies), Breasted (Egyptology), "Ajax" Carlson (physiology), Luckhardt (anesthesiology), Ricketts (for whom the rickettsial micro-organisms were named), Lillie (hormones), Quincy Wright (international relations), Tillich (theology), Paul Douglas (former Senator from Illinois), Merriam (political science), Kharasch (who developed the first seed disinfectant), or even predominantly undergraduate instructors like Schevill (history) and Herrick, Linn, Lovett, and Edith Foster Flint (English)? Who today can rival Dewey, Thorstein Veblen, or John B. Watson, who worked out his theory of behaviorism here? Why did the University lose giants like Vincent, Pound, and Angell? (Vincent became president of the University of Minnesota, and later head of the Rockefeller Foundation; Pound became Dean of the Harvard Law School; and Angell president of Yale, and later president of the Carnegie Foundation.)

This array of great names, of course, spans more than half a century of University history, and in any case the question is quite unfair. No university can indefinitely keep a man who, working there in his middle years, chooses to achieve the natural climax of his career elsewhere. And many of the titans now retired or dead were, as a matter of fact, succeeded by men just as distinguished but who did not happen to become campus legends. John A. Wilson, the Andrew MacLeish Distinguished Service Professor of Egyptology who has served as Director of the Oriental Institute and is now probably the most distinguished Egyptologist in the world, has a record fully equal to that of the great

Breasted. John A. Simpson has done work on space that puts him directly in the line of Michelson, Millikan, and other illustrious pioneers in physics.

That the University today possesses a faculty of the highest eminence is incontestable. The Physics Department was brutally hard hit by Fermi's death. Chemistry had to recover from Harold Urey's retirement, and Willard Libby's passage to a new field. But both continue as great departments. Anthropology is first class, Geography very strong, and Mathematics unsurpassed. Economics is a story in itself. Men like George J. Stigler hold strictly to the old laissez-faire line, but nobody can deny that they are vigorous and distinguished. Indic studies are extraordinarily strong—outstanding in the country—and so is Sociology. History is led by William H. McNeill, who was once an insurrectionary editor of the *Maroon*. McNeill has written an 829-page world history, *The Rise of the West,* which never mentions Churchill or Roosevelt and gives exactly one line to Adolf Hitler, but which has been praised by Toynbee as "the most lucid presentation of history in narrative form that I know"; and which in 1964 won the National Book Award for non-fiction.

David Riesman, author of *The Lonely Crowd,* taught at Chicago, and so did Dr. Frances Kelsey, an alumna who, moving on to a government job, won a well-merited presidential award by exposing the dangers accompanying the use of the tranquilizing drug thalidomide. Men and women of distinction are here by the score. Many are young and will become better known as years go by. It is invidious to mention some and omit others. I am doing no more than pluck a few flowers at random from a bouquet. One personage undeniably eminent is Mircea Eliade, the world's foremost scholar on primitive religions. Another eminent figure, with the somewhat difficult name of Subrahmanyan Chandrasekhar, in 1954 received from the Royal Astronomic Society of London its highest award, and is probably the world's most renowned astrophysicist. Hannah Arendt, whose academic title is Professor of Social Thought, has done brilliant work in the field of political philosophy, as well as controversial journalism.

Then, still picking at random, consider such men as Theodore W. Schultz (economics), Richard P. McKeon (philosopher and classicist), William H. Zachariasen (physics), and, among younger men, Humberto Fernández-Morán, a brilliant innovator in electron microscopy and space biology.

A dozen or so years ago "brain drain" took a good many distinguished scholars from the University, and morale on the faculty underwent a severe decline. Good men resigned left and right. But this trend has been sharply reversed. Nevertheless, the University still suffers normal losses. Alan Simpson, the highly regarded Dean of the College, became president of Vassar, and another top man, the statistician W. Allen Wallis, became president of the University of Rochester.

In a dozen fields Chicago scientists and scholars ceaselessly press against the frontiers of the unknown. Benson Ginsburg (genetics) has "socialized" a number of adult timber wolves, to find out whether wildness can be bred out of wild animals. Robert S. Mulliken, the Nobel laureate who is known as "Mr. Molecule," has done pioneer work on the separation of isotopes. Eugene Parker has proposed the existence of a "solar wind" which blows from the sun's corona, and several space scientists working under NASA grants are directing temperature studies of Venus and analyzing the surface of the moon. Edward Anders is one of the world's foremost authorities on cosmic dust.

Chicago's unrivaled record in the physical sciences is so well known that it scarcely needs further elaboration. Its scientists have participated in no fewer than twenty-five space satellite experiments. Willard F. Libby won a Nobel Prize partly for his work in formulating an atomic calendar by which the age of fossils and other relics could be specified through analysis of their radioactivity; this discovery has revolutionized archeology, and proves, among other things, the intricate interrelation of contemporary scholastic disciplines.

Glenn T. Seaborg, a Nobel Prize winner at the University of California, took a leave of absence from the Berkeley campus to serve with the Manhattan Project during the war years. At Chicago, Seaborg made history by measuring the mass of man's first artificially produced element—plutonium. On a closet-sized laboratory door in Kent Hall hangs a plaque commemorating this triumph. Other greats gathered at Chicago during this period were physicists Edward Teller, inventor of the H-bomb, and Eugene P. Wigner, who became a Nobel laureate in 1963. Harold C. Urey, who isolated heavy water and was another Nobel winner, and the late Leo Szilard, the brilliant Hungarian-born physicist, were long-time members of the faculty. Herbert L. Anderson, who came to Chicago as Fermi's assistant, has stayed on to gain distinction in high energy physics.

Then too consider the Biological Sciences. Chicago scientists have done notable work in fields from parasitology to trachoma to surgical shock, and the University spends $5.5 million annually (including the operations of Argonne Cancer Research Hospital) on cancer research. George Beadle, the President, is a Nobel Prize winner for his work on genes.

The overriding intellectual concern in research at Chicago is to answer basic questions and to solve bedrock quandaries. As Dean of the Division of Social Sciences at the University, economist D. Gale Johnson has, for example, assisted in the development of many research programs aimed at building up the storehouse of knowledge about mankind's social environment. But practical immediacies are not forgotten. For instance, James H. Lorie and Lawrence Fisher of the Graduate School of Business are engaged in the most complete analysis of the New York Stock Market ever undertaken, with a study of price movements since 1926.

In the Humanities, amongst much else, the University has been famous particularly for its work in lexicography. H. L. Mencken's *The American Language* has just been brought up-to-date by Chicago scholar Raven I. McDavid, and a computer has been put to work on the analysis of the ancient Hittite language. Chicago scholars (John Manly, Edith Rickert) produced years ago the definitive text of Chaucer's *Canterbury Tales,* and other professors made signal contributions to such fields as comparative philology (Carl D. Buck), and the Arthurian romances (William A. Nitze). No fewer than sixty-eight different languages, ranging from Akkadian to Urdu, are taught at Chicago, and the Oriental Institute has sent out more than forty-five expeditions since 1915. Chicago scholars have ranged as far as Chile (economics) and Basutoland (law). At home, campus scholars work on subjects as various as the *Federalist Papers,* early Chinese culture, and the papers of Addison and Steele. Robert J. Braidwood (Anthropology) is directing a long-range international expedition in southeastern Turkey, and Norman Golb (Medieval Jewish Studies) has discovered what happened to a Slovenian priest, by name Wecelinus, who renounced his Christian faith to become a Jew in the year 1005. Nobody ever knew what happened to him before. Finally in this general field, the *Encyclopædia Britannica* is published with the editorial advice of the faculties of the University of Chicago (and of a committee of members of the faculties of Oxford, Cambridge, and London universities and of a committee at the University of Toronto) by William Benton, one-time vice-president of the University and at present an indefatigable and spirited member of its Board of Trustees.

To summarize, it is the faculty which gives the University much of its unique quality, its special temper, based on a devout belief in research for its own sake and relentlessly acute and incessant speculation and experiments. The dominant principle is solid scholarship, and it demands the best.

Harper's Bazaar

Small principalities as well as large ones have their founding fathers, their historical *raison d'être*. The University of Chicago was founded in 1890 by the curious impingement of three forces—a Baptist organization (the American Baptist Education Society) which contributed the idea; John D. Rockefeller who contributed most of the money; and the first President, William Rainey Harper, who contributed almost everything else. It opened its doors on October 1, 1892, as a full-fledged university, not a college. This was something unusual at the time, when a university normally grew out of a previously existing college. The original faculty of 103 included eight college presidents, whom Harper enticed from other institutions, as well as other eminent scholars. The student body numbered 594.

Harper was one of the most extraordinary figures in the history of American education. He was a round, short, bristly man who radiated creative energy. At the time of his appointment he was Professor of Hebrew at Yale, and only 34. He had been a child prodigy (he got his Ph.D. at 18), Chautauqua lecturer, and an intellectual lion tamer at large. During his youth, which was spent in near log-cabin circumstances, he insisted that he was not a "Christian," but he became converted to the Baptist faith at the age of 20.

The Baptists urgently wanted a denominational school in Chicago to replace an older university which, founded in 1857, had been forced to close its doors by financial difficulties. For a long time the new university had a Baptist tinge. The President and two-thirds of the trustees were obliged to be Baptists, and one of the early jokes was that ambitious young deans should turn Baptist as soon as possible. But this Baptist coloration has long since disappeared, and the U. of C. is strictly non-denominational today.

Rockefeller, contrary to legend, was not gulled by Harper into making his original dramatic contribution, which was $600,000 on condition that $400,000 more should be raised elsewhere. Relations between these two men were fascinatingly complex. The demonic Harper, a whirlwind, captivated the cautious and rigid man who was the richest in the world. Rockefeller's bequests through the years became enormous. For many years, formal University stationery carried the rubric, "Founded by John D. Rockefeller." A grandson, David Rockefeller, board chairman of the Chase Manhattan Bank, got his Ph.D. at Chicago (his thesis was entitled "Unused Capital Resources and Waste") and remains an honorary trustee.

Harper, assuming charge of the creation of a new University, was enthralled by its possibilities; after being assured of getting a free hand, he issued an extraordinary manifesto of policy—a policy so revolutionary that it provoked the amusement or scorn of almost all the orthodox pedagogues of the time. First of all he announced that his institution would be primarily a graduate school. In addition, he went on to say that Chicago would abolish the old system of four classes and establish instead two colleges, the junior and the senior; he demanded equality of opportunity and treatment for women in the student body and on the faculty—this in an era when women teachers were almost unknown; a system of exchange professorships by which scholars all over the world would exchange courses with Chicago scholars; a system of extension work by which lectures under the auspices of the University would be given everywhere in the Middle West together with a system of affiliation with minor colleges; and an extensive correspondence school system. He even said that varsity sports should be played for health and pleasure, not "for the spectacular entertainment" of vast crowds. Obviously, his university was going to be like none other ever witnessed by the eyes of man. Rockefeller backed him fully, and covered immense deficits every year.

At this period the upper educational levels in America were dominated by the German concept of *Wissenschaft,* the scientific method. Harper wanted humanists, men of learning, men who would devote their whole lives to research with full freedom of inquiry. To get good men he paid salaries fantastic for the time—$7,000 a year to full professors, which was the equivalent of $30,000 today.

Soon this remarkable innovator and energizer evolved a novel idea which is still one of the most distinctive marks of the University—the four quarter system. He scrapped the old September-to-June schedule, and established in its place the first all-year-round university in the history of the world. The year was divided into four quarters which were made as nearly as possible identical in the work offered and the professors in attendance; the University was to keep its doors open the whole year, in full blast all the time. By this scheme University education was made more flexible than it had ever been before. A student—even today—may come when his finances permit, leave again, come back, and graduate at any season when his work is complete; on the other hand, he may work all four quarters for three years without interruption and thus get out a year ahead of time. Another advantage is that a student at Chicago takes no more than three or four courses during each quarter, and the curriculum is widened.

Harper's program was greeted with contumely and ridicule. One jokester called the new university "Harper's Bazaar," and there were loud complaints about the "oil money" supporting it. Once a professor at a rival institution was asked the reason for the absence of a humor magazine at Chicago; he replied that there was no need for one because the University of Chicago was funny enough in itself.

But—Harper's ideas worked. The University grew apace. More Rockefeller money poured in; more teachers came; more buildings rose. The campus grew up so fast that one of the early deans perpetuated a joke which is still current; "When in doubt lay a cornerstone."

Harper died, worn out, in 1906, aged 49. The University has never changed much from the pattern stamped on it by this extraordinary and indomitable man. There followed the deflationary, cautious, and comparatively tranquil presidency of Harry Pratt Judson (1907–23), followed in turn by two shorter administrations, those of Ernest De Witt Burton (1923–25), a theologian, and Max Mason (1925–28), a professor of mathematical physics, who went on to assume the presidency of the Rockefeller Foundation.

Then in 1929 came Robert Maynard Hutchins, aged 30, from Yale, where he had become the "boy wonder" Dean of the Law School at 28. The University will never forget Robert Hutchins, and discussion of his regime still provokes lively controversy. Hutchins was a brilliantly inspired innovator, lucid, packed with principle, and possessed of enormous charm. He is one of the most stimulating, courageous, and attractive men I ever met. He kept the faculty under merciless pressure, and has as little tolerance of opposition as Woodrow Wilson, whom he startlingly resembles in some respects. But he had—and has—a lively sense of humor. Laird Bell, a former chairman of the Chicago Board of Trustees, once offered him $25 for every joke he did *not* make when he was about to appear before the State Legislature.

But on things that counted Hutchins could be magnificently serious, as well as sound. Once, during a local "red" hunt when Professor Robert Morss Lovett was under attack by reactionary plutocrats, a fellow professor told him, "Bob, if the trustees fire Robert Lovett, you'll get twenty resignations from the faculty in twenty-four hours." Hutchins replied, "No, I won't. My successor will."

Hutchins' central belief was that "Every student should obtain a liberal education before being permitted to specialize." At the same time he wanted to speed up education so that work in the professions could get under way more quickly. What he sought was "more educated A.B.'s and fewer uneducated Ph.D's." He even looked forward, as somebody put it, to the time "when Ph.D's would really be Doctors of Philosophy." What interested him was ideas, and he stood for culture and the human tradition. Some of his innovations were remarkable—also unworkable. He wanted to do away with rank among professors, forbid them to earn money by their publications, and abolish examinations and required class attendance for students. He felt that education should be something bigger than a mere piling up of credits, and he let more air into American education than any university president in fifty years. Brave man, he even abolished football at Chicago.

The greatest date in the Hutchins period—and one of the great dates in the history of the world—was December 2, 1942, when Enrico Fermi produced the first controlled chain reaction and thereby initiated the atomic age. The scene was a converted squash rackets court under the stadium at Stagg Field, and assisting Fermi were a number of scholars including the late Leo Szilard and Arthur Compton, together with Harold Urey, Samuel K. Allison, and Herbert Anderson. The University had been working hard on what was then called "transuranic" chemistry and physics for a long time. The point had been reached where a full-scale nuclear pile, capable of a sustained chain reaction, had to be built if the Manhattan Project was to be a success, and the University of Chicago undertook to do this. Several industrial organizations and other universities had been approached by the government to construct the necessary but awesomely hazardous pile. They had refused to accept responsibility.

Hutchins had long been sympathetic to the isolationist position. He did not like the war. But he did not want to lose it. To decide to accept a mission which would presumably make practicable the production of an atomic bomb was surely one of the most onerous any man ever had to make, and Hutchins made it purely on his own. It had to be a dead secret, and the Stagg Field apparatus was erected and tested in total secrecy. The government has published a brief pamphlet describing the epochal events of December 2, 1942. The man who, at 3:25 P.M., pulled the cadmium rod out of the pile, under Fermi's direction, was named George Weil. An hour or two later Compton called President Conant at Harvard by long-distance telephone to inform him of the event. There had been no prearranged code, and Compton said merely, "The Italian navigator has landed in the new world." Conant replied, "How were the natives?" and Compton said, "Very friendly."

Soft Words and Shirtsleeves

The two men who have followed Hutchins as heads of state at Chicago came from quite different molds and have shown quite different styles. Happily, their talents have proved to be exactly appropriate to the University of Chicago's changing difficulties and challenges.

Lawrence A. Kimpton, an energetic professor of philosophy and a practical man as well who had become vice-president of the University, took over when Hutchins resigned in 1951, and served as chief executive until 1960. Persuasive, soft-spoken, a pre-eminent administrator, Kimpton's great contribution was his fruitful attack, intelligently conceived and executed with finesse, on the neighborhood problem which had come to curse the University, and he is the father of the urban renewal scheme which has vastly benefited the campus.

George Beadle, who succeeded Kimpton in 1961 to become the seventh president of the Chicago principality, is a biologist, a specialist in genetics, which is a field that could well turn out to mean to this generation what atomic physics meant to the last. Beadle, together with Joshua Lederberg and Edward L. Tatum, received the Nobel Prize in physiology and medicine in 1958. Beadle's and Tatum's work, to put it in the briefest terms possible, explored the nature of the behavior of genes and laid the foundation for modern biochemical (molecular) genetics.

Beadle has been called a "shirtsleeve man." Indeed his manner is informal, and one of his chief characteristics and sources of power is his modest likeableness. He speaks with a pronounced nasal twang, has a beguiling smile and, as I heard it put, "is instantly realizable to everybody." One of his colleagues told me that he has the finest of all gifts of a teacher, namely that he makes you think that you know what he knows. He doesn't lecture; he carries you along. Practically everybody on the campus has a part of George Beadle, and he is part of everybody. One teacher said of him, "He still acts as if he were a member of the *faculty!*"

Beadle's homespun touch is marked, although he certainly is not unsophisticated. He dislikes impedimenta. For instance he prefers to do his correspondence longhand. (His secretary has to snatch out important letters and repeat them on the typewriter for the record.) His view is long. He told me about one subject, "I dare say we'll know whether we were right about that twenty-five years from now." One of his characteristics is belief in reason. He can scarcely concede that two intelligent and honest people cannot reach agreement if a matter is fairly talked out. Yet he has a strong competitive instinct, and likes to win.

I had dinner one evening with him and Mrs. Beadle, a pleasantly astute and attractive woman, who has a strong interest in community problems, at the President's spacious Victorian-style residence. He had not had a wink of sleep the night before, because of a troublesome problem in University organization that was coming to a head. I asked him how he took the load off, how he relaxed after his usual 14-hour work day, and he replied, "I throw dirt." By this he meant that he likes gardening, and if he ever has a spare moment he digs in the back yard. If he has any other hobbies they are photography and mountain climbing. The Beadles have three Siamese cats of successive generations. One of these got stranded on the tall, steeply sloping roof of the President's house one day not long ago. Early risers in the neighborhood were startled to see George Beadle, President of the University, no less, climbing the roof barefoot at 6:00 A.M., roped to a friend whom he had summoned to help deal with this emergency.

Beadle was born in Wahoo, Nebraska, on October 22, 1903, and never had the faintest idea as a boy that he would be a university president. He wanted to be a farmer, and took his undergraduate major at the University of Nebraska in English. Presently he became interested in science—first entomology, then biology—and wrote his master's thesis on the identification of native grasses by characteristics other than their flowers. Beadle proceeded to Cornell, where he got his Ph.D. in 1931. His thesis there touched on what became his major work later: the interrelation of genes and chromosomes. Then he taught and studied variously at Caltech, Harvard, and Stanford, becoming in 1946 Professor and Chairman of the Division of Biology at Caltech. There he became Acting Dean and accumulated administrative experience.

Beadle has genuine gifts as a popular expositor and writes well, but it is not easy for a layman to grasp the detailed nature of the work for which he won the Nobel Prize. He was a pioneer in what has come to be called "cracking the genetic code," by which all known living creatures from viruses to man pass on their characteristics. His discovery, which was fundamental, was that genetic influences work through biochemical mechanisms, and may well lead in the future to developments whereby life itself may be created in the laboratory.

Chicago wooed Beadle away from the California Institute of Technology largely through the instrumentality of Glen A. Lloyd, then the Chairman of the U. of C. Board of Trustees. Beadle loved his home and work in California, but the challenge offered by Chicago overcame him. He visited the Midway and there met Edward H. Levi, then Dean of the Law School, who is one of the most persuasive men alive and who has an unfrightened attitude to the world. I asked Beadle how he had been able to tear himself away from the life of a scholar. "It was Levi who really hooked me," he said. Of course, Beadle had already been coaxed into administrative work at Caltech. And, after all, the presidency at Chicago is one of the highest academic appointments in the world.

During dinner at the Beadles' we were serenaded by a group of undergraduates protesting at the price of meals at Woodward Commons and the President, nicely assisted by Mrs. Beadle, handled this unexpected situation gracefully. He even made *me* say a few tranquilizing words. Students held forth posters with slogans like BIRTH CONTROL NOT FOOD CONTROL, END LEGALIZED MALNUTRITION, and BAN THE BUN, sang songs, and took a record of the proceedings with a portable recorder for subsequent use on the closed circuit campus radio. The University is nothing if not up-to-date. Incidentally, one of the student organizations fostering this event bears the name "Standing Committee to Rectify Unjustice," which resolves into the salty acronym SCRU.

Recovering from the amiable confusion of all this we talked a while after dinner mostly about neighborhood problems on which Mrs. Beadle is vividly articulate, and I asked Mr. Beadle a question, "Who runs the University?"

"My secretary, Doris Elaine Olson. She was Kimpton's secretary too. I asked her to stay on, and she said, 'Well, I'll give you a try.' "

Tablet presented by
the Class of 1911
Cres:
cat Sci
entia
Vita
Exco
latur

The Power Structure

Who does run the University of Chicago?

From trustees, faculty, students and outsiders, I got the same answer: "Under Beadle, Levi."

Edward Hirsch Levi, formerly Dean of the Law School, is Provost of the University and Beadle's right arm. One story about him is that his zeal and devotion to the University are such that for years he ate two lunches a day—one downtown seeing people who had to be seen, one on campus. Aristocratic, brilliant of mind, born of the best Jewish tradition (his maternal grandfather was the late Rabbi Emil G. Hirsch, the most renowned Jewish theologian in Chicago history), he has the interesting trait of being able to probe without arousing antagonism. His touch, his attitudes, his slight figure and flashing eyes, the mobility of his good looks, all indicate sophisticated refinement, but his record—he is an old Hutchins man—is that of a Young Turk.

Behind Beadle in the power structure are three major elements: trustees, faculty, and alumni. There have been only seven chairmen of the Chicago Board of Trustees in the entire history of the University, the same number as Presidents; at present the chairman is Fairfax M. Cone of the well-known advertising agency, Foote, Cone & Belding, a man marked not merely by broad creative talent but an acute and bold business mind. The Board has always represented the cream of Chicago civic leadership, and never has this been more true than today.

Several old-style Chicago tycoons had ambivalent feelings toward the University in older days. They respected it—perhaps stood in a certain awe of it—but they did not really like it. They thought that it was off-beat, radically inclined, even pinko, although its Economics Department is one of the most conservative in the country. But the old mercantile aristocracy could not abide its devotion to what they called the visionary. And the Irish political bosses thought that long-haired professors dedicated to theory were crazy. They were suspicious of anything "intellectual." Chicago has traditionally been "run" by State Street and the Irish (and other immigrant-descended) ward-heelers, and to most of these the University was a puzzle.

I dined several times with a number of the trustees. They do not deny that the University still has problems in the realm of community support. But no longer do Chicagoans on a serious level express hostility. Partly this is because of the influence of the trustees, one of the most courageous and independent-minded bodies of men ever to be associated with any university. They are men of money, but not hidebound. They have infinite faith in the University, and give it not merely efficient leadership but affectionate support.

Another point is that Chicago itself is changing. Its atmosphere is still brazen in some respects and it is a rough, gaudy city, but it is no longer "hog butcher to the world," as Carl Sandburg once characterized it. And nobody would write of it today as a city "inhabited by savages," as Kipling did. Its intellectual climate has broadened, and citizens tend steadily to understand better what an asset the University is—even if some still hesitate to send their children there.

The faculty has considerable autonomous power at Chicago, probably more than in any comparable American university. Beadle is faculty-minded, and so is Levi. (Provosts of universities are by no means always faculty-minded.) Harper laid it down back in the 1890's that educational jurisdiction is the exclusive domain of the faculty, and this tradition has been pretty well kept up to this day. The trustees do not supervise on the academic level. Money follows policy, not the reverse. The faculty is unshakeable. Even Hutchins had to bow to it, though his bow was angular. Mr. Beadle is fond of saying that he, as President, does not even have tenure, which every senior faculty member has, and one of his favorite anecdotes concerns the newly appointed president of another university who, on arrival, summoned the senior professors and addressed them as "my faculty." The reply came quickly, "Mr. President, faculties have presidents, but presidents do not have faculties."

The analogy should not be pushed too far, but the case might be made that Beadle is president of the Chicago principality, with Levi as his secretary of state; the Board of Trustees is the senate, and the faculty is the house of representatives. What I heard described as an "inner gerontology" probably still exists, but it does not wield serious power.

In terms of endowment Chicago is the fourth richest among private universities in the country; the total endowment is around $275 million, which produces a revenue of something between $9 and $10 million a year. But this is a drop in the bucket, since annual expenditures amount to $100 million, 68 per cent of which goes for instruction and research. Another $85 million is required to operate the Argonne National Laboratory, and this is contributed by the government. These are large sums and the University, like most other universities, is hard put to it these days to make ends meet, let alone find money for new purposes. And, as its fiscal authorities say, "The last million dollars in the budget is often the difference that makes possible exciting new developments."

Not remotely has the University been profligate. The Budget Committee of Trustees meets every two weeks and watches every cent. But for a long time Chicago sailed along under the comfortable impression that, being rich, it would always remain so. Then in recent years expenses rose sharply, as they have in every field. A new building costs $10 million instead of three or four, and upkeep—maintenance alone—is estimated at $3.00 per square foot a year, which in the case of a biggish building may run to $750,000. A single important new experiment in atmospheric physics, let us say, may cost $60,000 just for tools.

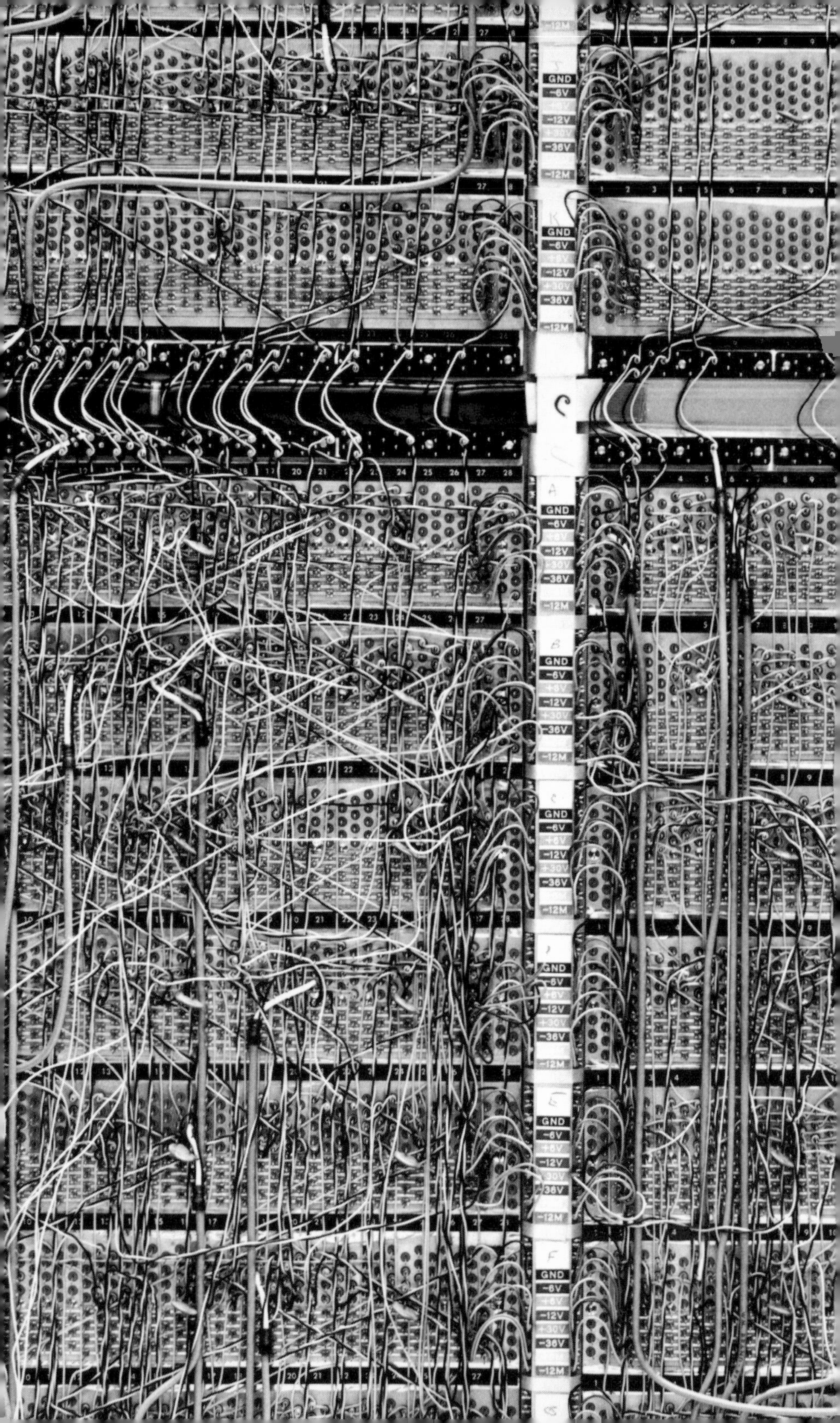

-12M
GND
-6V
+6V
-12V
+30V
-36V

An Academic Independence Fund

Especially in the world of academe, a principality must guard its economic independence if it is to remain intellectually free and viable. Not until I had strolled around the campus for several days did it occur to me that the most cardinal of all differences between the University in the 1920's and today is a factor that would not even have been dreamt of a generation ago—federal aid. During a recent year, government contracts for on-campus research at Chicago, exclusive of special projects such as the Argonne National Laboratory, had a value of $33,524,710. In other words, almost one-third of the University's expenditures are related to projects which the federal government believes are important enough to support with tax money.

Government support of university projects is useful, but Chicago would survive without it. And federal research money is a mixed blessing; it has produced certain almost invisible pressures on the faculty, which take two contrary directions. First, researchers operating under federal grants work under very substantial competitive pressure, and as a result may submit to the temptation to publish too early because the government wants results. Second, paradoxically, the federal authorities sometimes act as a brake on genuine creative activity because, generally speaking, government tends to play things safe.

This situation, which is duplicated in other universities all over the country, obviously poses problems. Inextricably, government has become involved in higher education everywhere in America to a degree and manner never known before. In its early days, Chicago depended almost entirely on private gifts, largely those made by Rockefeller and other individuals. Later foundations came to play a larger role. President Beadle, both as a scientist and an administrator, has done a good deal of hard thinking about the present situation, and observed recently:

"One often hears that government support means government control. It does not need to. First of all, we are a part of the government, and we have much to say about what it does and what it controls. If we do not say it loudly and clearly, we have no right to complain. Second, we have the option of accepting or not accepting support. . . . I suggest that in addition to exercising our right and obligation to advise the government, we can protect ourselves by keeping available sufficient uncommitted funds to enable us to say no to any proposal for government—*or private*—support that threatens our independence in an unacceptable way. I strongly favor the establishment of an 'independence fund' at the University of Chicago for just this purpose."

Beadle went on to speak of "one undesirable trend in universities that is accentuated by increased government support for research in areas of science and technology. That is a trend toward greater and greater salary differentials between scientists, mathematicians, and engineers on the one hand and social scientists on the other. . . . Many of us have responded to the competitive situation that exists by meeting market demands rather than by establishing honest and equitable salary scales based primarily on academic competence. Almost all major universities in this country have succumbed to the temptation, some reluctantly and sadly, and some, I am afraid, without quite realizing what they have been doing. I hope we can take corrective steps at the University of Chicago. It will not be easy."

Occasionally the University has minor tussles

with the government on a different level. When one government agency asked for the right to approve in advance the University personnel assigned to a training program in Pakistan, Chicago refused flatly to submit to this kind of supervision, and the government eventually backed down. In another case the government refused to withdraw a similar request; a deadlock followed and the project went to another university. But then a mild comeuppance came to the government because the other university invited a University of Chicago man to administer the operation.

Creating a New Community

Early in the 1950's came the greatest crisis in this academic sovereignty's history. It was caused by border clashes. The neighborhood problem reached such desperate intensity that the proposal—unbelievable as it may seem—was seriously considered of shutting the University down, or moving it out of Chicago. For several years the University of Chicago, with all its entrenched wealth and prestige, to say nothing of the constellation of scholars it had attracted, its record and achievements, was close to being destroyed, or having to destroy itself. Such a disaster would have been unprecedented in the history of American education.

For readers who do not know Chicago well a

word of background is necessary. The University is flanked by Lake Michigan and two pleasant parks, but to the north and northwest there lies an exposed frontier. This Hyde Park–Kenwood neighborhood, covering roughly 900 acres, was once one of the most fashionable in the city, but it began to deteriorate in the 1940's. It contained numerous houses, which still survive, where some of the early Chicago oligarchs lived in splendor in the 1890's, but the aristocracy moved out to take new positions on the North Shore and elsewhere and a wave of middle-class immigrants, mostly German and Polish, moved in.

Then, during World War II, a new enormous wave of immigrants swept into Chicago, seeking jobs in war industry. Mostly they were poor Negroes, but some of them were poor whites from the South. Neighborhood standards sank abruptly. Negroes then did not have the place in community life that many have today. In the 1940's the Hyde Park–Kenwood population (72,000) was six per cent Negro. But between 1950 and 1960 the proportion in Kenwood rose from ten to thirty-four per cent, in Hyde Park from three to thirty-eight per cent.

Most of the newcomers had nothing like the earning power or standard of literacy of the previous residents of the community. By 1952 the University area had the highest crime rate in the city, and citizens feared to go outside their houses after nightfall. The situation was much like that near

Central Park in New York City today. Muggings, robberies, assaults, burglaries took place. Soon this began to have a dire effect on the University. For some time it had been difficult to recruit promising young scholars—especially from abroad—because of surviving elements of the old Chicago "image," formed in prohibition days. Now the situation worsened. Not only did it become more difficult to recruit new men, but valuable professors quit. The student body shrank.

In short, the University found itself beleaguered. It was hemmed in. It was cut off by an atrocious belt of slum. Cheap cafés proliferated, and liquor bottles littered the streets. Speculators took to the habit of buying old buildings, cutting them apart and renting "apartments" to the poorest type of Negro, so that a structure originally built to hold one family might hold thirty or even forty people. Naturally, the buildings deteriorated while the landlords pulled in large profits. The problem was not a "Negro" problem per se, but rather one of Negroes on a miserably poor level of subsistence.

The first serious community efforts to deal with this situation had their genesis in 1949. Herbert A. Thelen, then an Assistant Professor of Education (and now a full professor) at the University, organized block work. He and other faculty members helped bring about, on February 1, 1950, at a mass meeting in the community house of Temple Isaiah Israel, the formation of the Hyde Park–Kenwood

Community Conference. The hat was passed, and $127.25 was collected to inaugurate a community rehabilitation project which—nobody even dreamed then—would ultimately come to cost nearly $200 million.

The grievous neighborhood problem came to a head soon after Kimpton became Chancellor of the University. He faced the facts squarely and accepted it that "the University's very survival was at stake." He pointed out that a university could be made or broken in a decade, "a terrifying thought," and said that "we are fighting for our lives." There seemed to be three alternatives: (1) submit to accelerating processes of decay, (2) fight, (3) sell out. This latter alternative was seriously considered. But this would have meant the sacrifice of a campus of which the physical installations alone were worth at least a quarter of a billion dollars, and to which more than $330 million had been contributed in seventy years. Moreover, as it was cogently put, "Nothing is less saleable than a university campus." "There is not much market," added one trustee grimly, "for a secondhand university." One proposal was to move out of the city into the Argonne area; another was to hop to California and merge with Stanford.

It took courage, realism, and imagination to decide, instead, to fight. Once the decision was made, Kimpton and the trustees surveyed the ground—literally. The cost to the University was estimated at $30 million. But to save itself, the University had to become a major force in the struggling community effort to save the neighborhood as well. The whole Hyde Park–Kenwood area had to be cleared up, and the only way to do this—unprecedented!—was to make it a stable interracial community. And this was done.

Kimpton was destined to provide much of the leadership in this remarkable undertaking, but as President of the University he could not devote all his energies to it. The day-to-day direction was assumed by an indefatigable, tough-minded lawyer named Julian Levi, brother of Edward, and now a member of the faculty. If Edward is a poniard, Julian is a sledgehammer. First he sought to arrest forces making for decay. He went after the slumlords with fierce and weighty determination, getting judgments against them for the illegal conversion of buildings and the like. He not only used the courts but went around the corner to persuade insurance companies to cancel their coverage on tainted buildings, or the mortgage holders to demand immediate repayment.

The Hyde Park–Kenwood Community Conference was already two years old when, following a mass meeting at Mandel Hall on the campus in 1952, a second organization came into being named the South East Chicago Commission. Kimpton took the presidency of this, and Julian Levi became director. It came close to being a vigilante organization. Residents of the area watched and reported on anything suspicious—for instance the arrival at a site of unusual loads of lumber or crates holding an undue number of washbasins, which might mean that a building was about to be illegally converted.

Levi worked patiently—and impatiently—on political and legal levels. Every pertinent law on the books, municipal, state and federal, was utilized. A relentless spotlight on the profits of slum speculators even brought about convictions and jail sentences for tax evasion. Finally the decision to rehabilitate the neighborhood became practicable, and city, state, and federal funds became available, particularly after passage of the Federal Housing Act of 1954. The City of Chicago, under Mayor Richard J. Daley, cooperated handsomely.

In 1954 a group of buildings was acquired and demolished in an area covering forty-eight acres in Hyde Park. The land was cleared and an entirely new community created on a multi-racial basis—including an elaborate shopping center, two apartment buildings with 550 units, and about 250 town houses. Elsewhere in the neighborhood, areas totaling 591 acres, on which stood more than 3,000 buildings containing nearly 30,000 living units, were designated for renewal. More than 600 buildings were torn down and 101 acres were cleared. Rebuilding and rehabilitation of existing buildings has been going on ever since.

Since no public money was available until 1954, the campaign had to rely entirely on private contributions at the outset. Marshall Field gave $100,-000, thus carrying on a family tradition; it was his grandfather who donated to the University some of its first land. The contribution of the University so far to the project as a whole has been about $30 million, out of a total cost of $250 million. Results have made the adventure, expensive as it was, undeniably and thoroughly worthwhile, and acres of vicious slum disappeared.

This was not only a pioneer job in urban renewal but it is still one of the two or three biggest and most elaborate ever undertaken in the country. Crime has gone down by a third, tax collections are up, and the community is not only prosperous but tranquil. Only a small percentage of the affected people suffered. A new savings and loan association has been chartered whose depositors and mortgagors are avowedly interested in fostering the kind of interracial neighborhood the University community has become. The chief point to emphasize is of course the enduring interracial characteristics of the rebuilt area. Whites and Negroes are becoming fairly well interspersed, although much still remains to be done.

I had dinner with Provost Levi one evening; I watched the children of his next-door neighbor playing in the adjacent yard—a Negro family. One trustee I met lives in an integrated apartment building, with Negroes as his fellow tenants as a matter of course. Negroes sell property to whites; whites sell property to Negroes. An effort is being made to persuade whites to buy property in pockets still predominantly Negro—"managed integration." To sum up, the new area is probably the stablest interracial community in the United States—volatile no longer.

The Negro population of Hyde Park–Kenwood as a whole is now forty per cent. This is up two per cent from 1956—sufficient answer to the charge that Negroes have been "renewed-out" of the community.

And the University has been saved.

Unfrightened and Pertinacious

After ten days in the remarkable Chicago principality I said good-bye to its towers and meadows and tried to analyze my dominating thoughts. Perhaps the single element that best characterizes the University is its incessant search for quality, which goes back all the way to Harper. If a case need be made for the private urban university in our contemporary life, surely Chicago makes it. Between the Atlantic and Pacific it towers like a lonely colossus, symbolizing the aspirations and achievements of one of the most fruitful areas of our country, the Middle West. Quality aside, this is a school which stands for freedom of expression, freedom to speculate and experiment, freedom for spacious inquiry, freedom to be a gadfly if necessary, and freedom not only to be right but to take a chance on being wrong. It does not have to kowtow to any legislature or city council, although its relations both with Springfield and City Hall are excellent. It has unlimited reserves of energy and creative talent for dealing with the true business of a university, the pursuit and communication of knowledge, and, having survived a passionate ordeal, it has risen again to become newly typical of what a university should be, an unfrightened and pertinacious community of scholars. It still has its unique atmosphere of vitality and gives forth a sense of endurance as well as youth. My own feeling is that it is still the most exciting university in the world.

Sources

Predominantly my sources have come by word of mouth. But I should mention too my debt to a small shelf of written material, including numerous catalogues, pamphlets, and documents put out by the University. Also:

BEADLE, GEORGE W. "The New Genetics," *Britannica Book of the Year, 1964.*

BEADLE, MURIEL. *The Hyde Park–Kenwood Urban Renewal Story, 1949–64.* Berkeley Community Enlightenment Lines, 1964.

DOBBINS, CHARLES G. (ed.). *The University, The City and Urban Renewal.* American Council on Education, 1964.

KERR, CLARK. "The Multiversity," *Harper's Magazine,* November, 1963.

LEVI, JULIAN. *The Neighborhood Program of the University of Chicago,* 1961.

MANLY, CHESLEY. "A report on the University of Chicago," *Chicago Tribune,* 1961, and a similar report (1963) by various *Chicago Tribune* correspondents.

MAYER, MILTON. *Young Man in a Hurry: The Story of William Rainey Harper.* University of Chicago Alumni Association, 1957.

MAYER, MILTON. "Hutchins of Chicago," *Harper's Magazine,* March and April, 1939.

For the section on Hutchins I have cannibalized a few passages from my *Inside U.S.A.* (1947) and I have also used a paragraph or two from an article I wrote for the old *Smart Set* when I was an undergraduate.

I want to thank cordially several Chicago friends who helped me as well as members of the Board of Trustees and faculty. In particular my debt is high to George W. Beadle, Fairfax M. Cone, Carl Larsen, Director of the Public Relations Office of the University, and Mrs. M. J. Carlson, his associate.

J. G.

EARLE LUDGIN

How It Began

It is not generally known, I am sure, that John Gunther came to the University expecting to major in Chemistry. Required to take courses in English composition, he came into the hands of Mrs. Edith Foster Flint, and soon changed direction from the north campus to the south. I don't know whether James Weber Linn was in on the conversion or merely confirmed it later. John became one of his favored friends and students. Anyone who met Browning and the other poets in Mr. Linn's company found English literature and the English language, in the words of a later poet, "charged with the grandeur of God." John gave up all thought of Chemistry.

John's career really began on the *Maroon*. He

began by contributing book reviews which were thoughtful, mature and readable. Then John added another dimension. He interviewed the authors who came to the University to lecture or to teach, and wrote feature articles for the *Maroon*. It may be said that his interviewing technique developed in this period.

While still on campus, Gunther developed friendships among newspapermen, principally on the *Chicago Daily News*. He lunched at Schlogl's in the company of Carl Sandburg, Ben Hecht, editor Henry Justin Smith, and Harry Hansen. Soon he was writing book reviews for the *News*, as well as for the *Maroon*. If he didn't get paid, at least he kept the books, and soon was extraordinarily well read in contemporary writing.

Then came the next step. Gunther was invited to interview visiting literary celebrities for the *Daily News*, and some of his columns actually appeared on the front page of the paper while he was still a student.

It was natural for John, on graduation, to go to work for the *Daily News*. His aim was clear. He wished to join the famous foreign service of the *News*, but when he applied for an assignment in Europe he was turned down because seniority governed such appointments. John quit and went to Europe on his own. He carried with him letters of introduction to all the literary lions in England, many of whom he had met in Chicago.

In London, he applied at the *News* office there for a job and was given a temporary one to fill in for a vacationing member of the staff. When that term was up, John was given a chance to fill in at other *Daily News* offices on the continent and then he landed with considerable permanency at Vienna. It was an anxious time in Europe, and many roads led to Vienna.

Gunther filed his stories with regularity. He is an assiduous worker, who briefs himself with every available fact before he undertakes an assignment. Then he took time to write some articles for *Vanity Fair*. John began to look at history-in-the-making through the men who were making it. The interviewing technique that he developed on the *Maroon* came to full flower. Through his position as a foreign correspondent for a great American newspaper and through his own pertinacity, he managed to meet anyone of importance.

Later he was to gather these character drawings into his first book, *Inside Europe*. He had devised something more than journalism, closer to contemporary history. The device was quite his own.

It all started when a former student of Chemistry changed to an English Major and began interviewing literary celebrities for the *Maroon*.

Earle Ludgin is a member of the Board of Trustees. He was a contemporary of Mr. Gunther at the College and is presently Chairman of the Board of Earle Ludgin & Co., a Chicago public relations and advertising firm.

Photographic Captions

All photographs are by David Windsor.

Published by
The University of Chicago
May, 1967